The Actors Handbook

The Actors Guide to Conquering Hollywood

By Rebecca Robinson

Minute Help Press

www.minutehelp.com

© 2011. All Rights Reserved.

I0430161

Table of Contents

Introduction

Every year thousands of people make their way to Southern California ready to take on the world and become the next big thing in Hollywood. We have all heard the stories of the young actor or actress who was discovered shortly after arriving in town and became a star. Hollywood likes those stories; they perpetuate the dream that, deep down, so many of us share.

Can it happen that quickly? Yes… it can happen that quickly.

Will it happen that quickly? Don't count on it.

After reading this guide you will know two things that most of your competition does not.

How the entertainment industry in Hollywood REALLY works.

What you can do to have an advantage over almost everyone else.

We are here to bust myths and share truths. This is the best information from those INSIDE the industry. If you want a career in Hollywood, take notes.

Chapter 1: Living in Los Angeles

The first challenge actors face when arriving in Los Angeles is… well, Los Angeles. The Los Angeles metropolitan area is not the easiest area for newcomers. Everything from the smog, to the traffic, to apartments that may not come with refrigerators can be shocking for those new to the city. The best course of action is to do research and plan ahead before you make the leap. Some of the things you must figure out before you arrive include:

Where will you stay when you first get there – If you have friends or family you can stay with when you first arrive, this is the way to go. If this is not an option, you will want to research hotels or short-term apartments where you can stay temporarily.

Transportation

Do you need a car to survive in Los Angeles? No. People often have the perception that there is no available public transportation in L.A. In fact, the Metro system of buses and trains makes it possible to get to the majority of the popular areas. That said, you will WANT a car in L.A. if at all possible. Things are very spread out and you can't get everywhere you want by Metro.

Money

You will need to find a job to pay the bills when you get to L.A., but you will also need to have enough money to survive until you get your first paycheck. Don't show up in town with $100 in your pocket.

Apartment Hunting

Okay, so now you are in Los Angeles. In order to stay for more than a few weeks you will need an apartment. If you are from a smaller town or city you may be surprised at the costs of rent in L.A. You will have a hard time finding a decent one-bedroom apartment for under $1,000. You want to choose a location that is close enough to where the entertainment industry is focused; which is primarily Hollywood, West Hollywood, and the E. San Fernando Valley.

This leaves quite a few areas that you can consider when apartment hunting. A couple of areas that are popular with actors are Studio City and Toluca Lake. Both areas are very diverse and offer a wide variety of restaurants and places to hang out. Hollywood is relatively affordable, but it has a very urban feel that is not for everyone. West Hollywood is more expensive and trendier than Hollywood. In the Westside part of L.A. there are some very desirable areas, such as Westwood and Santa Monica. While these are very popular areas they are typically very expensive. A better budget option in the area is Culver City.

There are numerous ways to locate apartments in L.A. You can search classified ads in the Los Angeles Times as well as local papers in individual towns. Online options such as Craigslist can be a good resource, but Craigslist is also known for scams, so be careful. Driving around neighborhoods can be an excellent way to find something that might not even be advertised. Talk to anyone and everyone you meet. You never know who will hear about a great place to live.

If money is very tight the best option may be to share an apartment with one or more roommates. There are a number of roommate agencies. Listings at universities are also a great resource to find roommates. The roommate option may also be the best option if you have not yet established credit.

A common theme you will encounter in this guide is to have a plan. When it comes to living in L.A. planning ahead is the key to a smooth transition.

Chapter 2: Actor Training

One of the questions prospective actors often ask is whether or not they need training. For actors without many (or any) credits on their resume the answer is a definite yes. There are a number of reasons why training is so important for the actor just starting out.

It matters to casting directors - When you don't have a lot of experience you need to do something to show the people who can hire you that you are serious about the business. There are so many young people who enter the business and think that they will get jobs because of their looks and charm. Casting directors want to meet with (and hire) people who are skilled professionals. The best indicator of this (outside of actual work experience) is someone who has made the commitment to further their acting education. Casting directors have been very open about their feeling on the subject; training is important.

It makes you feel like an actor – When you first start out and (most likely) are not working as an actor it can be energizing to be around similarly passionate people. The fact that it can help you hone your craft and actually become a better actor should also not be overlooked.

It's important to network – A recurring theme in this guide will be the importance of building relationships. Acting classes are a great way to meet new people who are in the industry.

You will find no shortage of acting classes in the Los Angeles area. Every industry publication you read or website you visit will have advertisements for classes. Everyone you meet will have their favorite teacher or class. You want to find a teacher that will let you audit the class. You cannot be sure that the vibe of the class is right for you until you see it in person. A great teacher for one person may not be the right one for another. Talk to some of the students in the class. If possible, go for coffee or a drink after the class. Students are often more honest about their thoughts when they are not in the school environment.

Make sure that the acting philosophy of the school is something that works for you. Does the school focus on theory, scene study, the business side of the industry, or some combination of these subjects? Do they have showcases, or invite industry professionals to speak to the students?

Find out how your experience and previous training compare to the other students in the class. Ask about the time commitment, both during and outside of the class. You want to know exactly what is expected of you and how you will be evaluated within the class. How will your progress be measured? Is the class ongoing, or for a set time period?

It is a buyers' market for acting classes in L.A. There are plenty of good ones and you don't need to spend a fortune. Below I have listed a few popular schools to get you started. Shop around a bit and you will easily find one that meets your needs.

- The Groundlings School
- The Lee Strasberg Institute
- Howard Fine Acting Studio

Chapter 3: The Business of Hollywood

There are a number of myths about how actors find work in Hollywood. Don't limit yourself or your opportunities because you have been given bad information.

Myth Number #1

You Need an Agent to Get Work

This is simply not true. It is a myth that has been perpetuated in the industry, probably by agents who make a lot of money by getting their 10% from actors. Don't get me wrong, an agent can be very important and can absolutely help take your career to the next level. But they are not necessary to find work. The primary role of an agent (more on this later) is to find out about and submit you for auditions. The truth is that you can do much of this work yourself. This is particularly true for some of the smaller scale projects that you are likely to be considered for early in your career.

Reading industry publications such as The Hollywood Reporter, Variety, and Backstage West will provide tons of information about projects in various stages of development. There are also some fantastic sites such as actors access that make breakdowns (summaries of plot and the available roles) of the different projects available to actors. For a small fee per submission, actors access allows actors to submit electronically for a large number of projects. You can send casting directors headshots, resumes, and even video. A better value for some people is a subscription to Showfax. Showfax makes sides (parts of scripts) available to actors to study before auditions. If you subscribe to Showfax (currently $68 per year) you are able to submit through actors access for free. If you plan to do a lot of electronic submissions (and you should), this is a great value.

Myth Number #2

You need to be a Member of SAG to Get Work

Once again, wrong, wrong, wrong. Not only is this not true; the truth is for most people joining the Screen Actors Guild early in their career is a very bad idea.

First of all it is expensive to join SAG. Current membership dues are over $2,000 for the first year. In addition to this, once you are a member of the union you will not be able to work on non-union projects. Early in your career it is likely you will want and need to work on non-union projects. Far too many people jump at the first chance they get to join SAG and don't consider how it can limit their options for work.

There is also a common misperception that you can't work on a union project if you are not a member of SAG. Once again, this is not true. SAG has lots of rules stating how this happens depending on the size of the project, but rest assured, if someone wants you to be in their film, they will not care that you are not in the union. They will get SAG the paperwork they need and you will be in the film. It's that simple.

Finding work in Hollywood is not easy, but it is also not as daunting as you are led to believe. In the coming sections we will go further into the process of getting work and ultimately, you will have a complete plan of action.

Marketing Yourself

A Few Things You Must Do

Any actor who hopes to have a career in Hollywood needs to have marketing materials that present the image of a polished professional. The standard tools of the trade have long been the headshot and resume. These are still the most important, but a professional video reel is expected today as well. In this section we will go over the best advice for putting together these critical pieces.

Headshot

The headshot is the first thing that agents, casting directors, and everyone else views. It is your business card and it has to say what you want it to say. The most important element of the headshot is that it looks natural. The last thing you want is a picture that looks like you were posing for a picture. Ideally, you would like to have a shot that communicates your personality. Think about what reaction you want from those who view the picture. If should be consistent with the "type" of roles that you are auditioning for.

One point that cannot be overstated is that your headshot MUST look like YOU. The quickest way to tick off a casting director is to walk into the meeting or audition looking nothing like your picture. This means that not only do you have to update your shots as often as necessary (typically every 3-5 years), but your hair and makeup in the picture should be consistent with your normal everyday look.

In L.A. headshot photographers are their own industry. You will have plenty of choices to choose from. Unfortunately, most of them will be very expensive. You can pay anywhere from a few hundred to a few thousand dollars for a professional headshot photographer.

Those who do not have the budget for a professional photographer still have options. Fortunately for the actor, digital photography is a lot more forgiving than film. If you or someone you know has a decent digital camera try to have a friend take the pictures. There are plenty of videos on YouTube offering advice on how to use lighting to get the most flattering picture. It doesn't matter if you take 1,000 bad shots; all you need is one good one.

Another option is to seek out photography students from professional programs. They are often looking to build their own resume, and may do the shoot for free or at a very low cost.

When having the prints made you don't need to go crazy with the most expensive paper. Find something that looks neat and professional and that should be fine. If you shop around you will find better values.

In addition to the standard 8X10 headshot, many actors choose to have smaller photo postcards created. These are used to send personal notes to casting directors or others. It is a personal touch that helps to keep your name and face on their radar.

Resume

Most resumes are printed directly on the back of the headshot.

Your name should go at the top of the resume, with any union affiliations directly under the name. Next should be your contact information, including cell phone and website (if any).

The credits section is the main body of the resume. List credits by order of prestige, NOT chronologically. The order of prestige is typically film, followed by television, and then theater. If you don't have any professional experience, focus on any school or community theater productions.

Underneath the credits section list all of the professional training you have had. If you have a university degree in a relevant subject that should be listed as well.

The final section should be any special skills that may be relevant, such as dialects or stage fighting.

You should not put very personal information such as your address or social security number on the resume. There is also no need to put your weight or exact age.

The goal of your resume is to highlight your most impressive and noteworthy achievements. Ideally you want to include enough information to impress the reader, but not give so much that they feel as if they know everything about you. If you do a quick internet search you will find many samples of what this can look like.

Video

The final piece to your marketing arsenal should be the video reel. Many new actors do not have any video to create a reel. As soon as possible do a few student or low budget films and get some content to create a video. It is a very useful tool that lets casting directors see you in action.

Talent Agents

Earlier in the guide, I mentioned that you do not need a talent agent to find work. Why then, does it seem that the primary concern of every actor is, "how do I get a good agent?" The truth is that the right agent, at the right time, can be a very important asset to the actor.

To fully understand the value that an agent can bring to an actor we need to step back and discuss what talent agents do. The primary job of an agent is to find auditions for an actor, handle the negotiating of the contracts, and be an advocate for their client when disputes may arise. Talent agents may have many clients, a few clients, or no clients at all. They may work for large and powerful agencies, smaller agencies or be on their own. Just as there are struggling actors trying to break into the business, there are also struggling agents trying to do the same thing. All legitimate talent agents are licensed and bonded by the state of California.

While many actors are anxious to find any agent at all it is very important to not fall into this trap. A bad agent can be much worse than no agent at all. Most actors would like to believe the portrayal of the agent as the friend and mentor, tirelessly working to help their client succeed, no matter what it takes. The reality is that the job of the agent is to make money. As long as you are the one making them money things will be great. As thousands of actors can testify, when the bookings dry up, often the agent relationship does as well. Actors typically believe that it is the job of the agent to find them work. Agents usually don't see it this way. They usually take the position that only those actors who regularly win jobs (and produce commission) are worth spending time on.

When you do find the right agent, the one that makes you a priority, you will have access to a larger and more prestigious selection of jobs. While actors access and similar services do offer breakdowns for many projects, the reality is that most of the larger and union projects are not made available to the actor. They are only available to agents who subscribe to breakdown services targeted specifically to agents. Furthermore, as your career advances a good agent will be able to negotiate better salary and perks than you would for yourself.

How Do I Find an Agent?

The standard line in Hollywood is that you do not find an agent, "they find you." There is some truth to this. The search for an agent can bring to mind the old Groucho Marx quote about not wanting to "belong to a club that accepts people like me as members." The agents that you want to meet with won't talk to you and the agents that will talk to you make your skin crawl. So how exactly does one go about getting an agent? Some of the most common strategies include:

Direct mailing – Some actors have found agents simply by sending them a headshot/resume and cover letter. For a couple of reasons, this isn't the best strategy for most people. First, and most importantly, it isn't very effective. Yes, you do hear the occasional story of the actor who found an agent this way, but it is very rare. Most agents admit that they don't even look at unsolicited submissions. The other point to consider is that it can get very expensive. If money is no object, there is no reason not to do it; but for most people it's not a good use of resources.

Referral from a Casting Director – A method that has had better results than direct mailing agents involves asking casting directors for agent recommendations. Right about now, you are probably thinking… great, but I don't know any casting directors either. While getting meetings with casting directors can also be challenging, for many actors it proves to be easier than reaching agents. Casting agents often attend workshops and showcases and generally engage the general acting population more than agents. They are often happy to help actors that they like.

Stay Busy – The most common way to find an agent is to simply be seen doing quality work. You should be working as often as possible. This can include student films, live theater, and even public workshops. If you consistently do good work, word will get out. You can even target a few agents and invite them to see your performance.

If you get a meeting with an agent remember that the thing he is most concerned with is whether or not you can make him money. You have to appear professional and formidable. Be humble, but confident. You probably won't need it, but have a monologue or two ready just in case. You should, of course, have a hard copy of your headshot and resume, along with a copy of your DVD reel.

They love me... now what?

So the stars have aligned and the agent of your dreams actually wants to sign you to a contract. What happens next? An agent will probably ask you to sign a GSA, which is a general services agreement, as well as the standard SAG agent's agreement. The GSA, which is regulated by the state of California, typically covers a longer period of time and allows the agent both a higher percentage and a portion of additional income that they don't get under the SAG agreement. If this sounds a little confusing (and it should), it only illustrates why it is critical at this point to have any and all contracts looked over by an entertainment lawyer. This is a VERY important step. The small cost that you pay for this will be worth every penny.

Many actors are so excited when an agent agrees to represent them that they will sign anything put in front of them. Do not fall into this trap. A professional agent will respect you for protecting your interests. It is an unfortunate reality that there are agents that are not reputable or honest. When looking for an agent, keep in mind the thought that if it seems too good to be true, it probably is. If an agent asks for any money up front, or requires you to use his photographer or any other service, run like the wind. Legitimate agents never do this. Stay busy and follow the recommendations given here and you will eventually find an agent.

Chapter 4: Casting

Though we have alluded to certain parts of the casting process in this guide, it is important to have a complete understanding of what actually happens when casting a project.

The process starts when the casting director sends out the breakdown. As we mentioned earlier, the breakdown is a brief synopsis of the plot with a listing of the different roles that are to be cast. The casting director may send this out to a variety of locations. Breakdowns may go out to sites like actors access and similar services such as LA Casting. They may also be found in industry magazines such as Backstage West among others. Often times, for the most prestigious union projects, the only breakdowns will go to a breakdown service that provides them solely to agents.

When the agents receive the breakdowns, they (hopefully) notify their actors of roles that they are suitable for. They will also submit the actors' information, including headshot/resume, and often video reel. This is usually done on the same day that the listing was posted. Actors who do not have agents (and even those who do) should carefully search all of the online resources to find breakdowns that interest them. Many different casting directors have stated that submitting early is an advantage, particularly for those without agents. Anyone who gets their information submitted on the first day has an advantage. Later submissions often do not even get looked at. As we have discussed, submitting electronically is simple thanks to actors access.

It should be noted that while the vast majority of submissions are now done electronically, some projects may indicate that they do not want electronic submissions, or would like a hard copy in addition to the electronic submission. It is very important that the submission has a professional look. No brown manila envelopes. Use a professional looking white or cream envelope with all addresses typed on the envelope.

Every time you communicate with people in the industry, whether in person or through correspondence, you have an opportunity to show your professionalism. If this seems like it shouldn't matter, remember there are real people on the other end. Whether conscious or not, they are forming an opinion about you before you even meet. It's this attention to detail that helps you to stand out from thousands of other people.

Unfortunately, there are bound to be some breakdown listings that are not legitimate. The rules of common sense must apply. All breakdowns have detailed information about the project. The less information provided, the more dubious the listing is likely to be.

Often within a few days of posting the breakdown the casting director will make the choices of actors to bring in for an audition. If you have an agent they will go through the agent. If you are on your own, they will contact you directly. Now comes the fun part; it's time to get ready for the audition.

Auditioning

The audition is the single most important event in the life of the actor. The more you know about the process the easier and less mysterious the auditions will become. You will still get nervous, but you will be prepared.

Who is this mysterious casting director?

We have previously mentioned the casting director in this guide; but who exactly is the casting director and what is their responsibility? The casting director may work for the studio, but they are often independent employees. Like so much of Hollywood, the job of casting director is very competitive. They know they can be fired at any time. They really don't have any significant power in the production. They will not make final decisions about casting. They may be asked for their opinion, and with the nature of relationships, some will have more influence on particular projects, but they do not have ultimate casting power. The power that casting directors have is over actors. They are the ones that get us in the door.

It's important to keep in mind the perspective of the casting director. They have a job to do and anyone who makes that easier gets on their good side. Conversely, any actor that shows up late, unprepared, or not looking like their headshot will have created an enemy that they likely will keep for a very long time. And remember this, all of Hollywood talks, and casting directors are no exception. If you appear unprofessional in any way, word will spread; and you will have a very difficult time getting more auditions. It may seem cruel, but it actually offers a significant advantage for those who understand how things work. By being a pro from beginning to end you will be remembered for the right things; whether you get this job or not.

You Are Always Being Evaluated

From the moment you walk into the audition waiting room and sign in you are being scrutinized. Never forget this. How you treat the audition monitor as well as the other actors in the room may all be considered. You should be respectful and friendly to the audition monitor; but not too friendly. This can be perceived as sucking up. It is always a fine line; if you are just yourself and genuinely polite you will come across well. Never complain when waiting and please do not talk on your cell phone. Now would be a good time to turn your cell phone off. When you are called in to the audition room you may get nervous and forget to turn it off. You DO NOT want your phone to ring during your audition.

When you are called into the audition room, walk in confidently, but not arrogantly. You should have a welcoming look on your face like you are eager to meet those in the room. This works best if you actually feel this way, but if not… well, you are an actor.

Do not walk into the room in character. Try to remember that these people are evaluating you as a person as much as they are looking at your acting. As one casting director put it, "we will be spending a lot more time with the actor than with the character." This is a critical point that almost all actors miss during the audition. Yes, it's true that if there is one absolute perfect choice that stands out above all others, you probably won't get the job because the casting director likes you. However, if there are five people who are being considered, you better believe what they think of you as a person matters. These decisions are not being made by computers. They're real people with real emotions.

Give them a chance to get to know you. Make sure you look people directly in the eye when you talk to them. If they don't tell you, politely ask who you will be reading with. Give a genuine smile to that person and say something like "great", or "cool" - whatever comes naturally to you.

You Are Pretty Much on Your Own

If you are expecting to receive helpful and illuminating casting direction from the casting director... think again. You will be reading for the casting director and probably a few associates. They are not actors and they are not directors, they are casting directors. While they may think that they have given you some brilliant insight into the character and scene, you will probably feel differently. It is what it is. The good news is that it is the same for everyone. No one auditioning is getting better direction than you are. One of the essential skills of the audition process is being able to nail the material without the benefit of masterful direction.

You should have received the sides (part of script) from either your agent, or if you don't have an agent you could have gotten it from Showfax or directly from the casting director. There is no excuse for not being prepared. You will be expected to know the script and be ready to read. Unless you have had the sides for an extended period of time (at least a week) you probably won't be expected to memorize every line. If you are great at memorizing, it will take some pressure off; but otherwise don't sweat it too much. Refer to the script as needed. That is perfectly fine. No one will think less of you for it.

There will be a camera or two in the room. Do not read to the camera. Interact with the person you are reading with. Some people find that taking a class that teaches auditioning technique helps them to feel more at ease with the dynamic of the room. It couldn't hurt to sit it on a class to see if it is something you think would be helpful.

When you are finished reading during your audition, you should stop and be quiet. Don't say "scene," and don't make a joke. You may feel the urge to do this, which comes from the release of tension when you are done. Resist the temptation. Simply thank everyone in the room and prepare to calmly and confidently walk out. They will appreciate your professionalism. Rest assured, if they want you to stay for any reason they will let you know. One last thing, DO NOT ask about callbacks. Once again, they will let you know in time if you will be getting a callback.

Did someone mention Callbacks...?

If you do get a call back the process will be similar to the first audition, with them contacting either your agent or you. The actual audition will most likely have the director and producer sitting in. Don't try to figure out what they want. Your instincts were good the first time. Follow the same protocol from the first audition. Within a few days you should get word of their decision.

Chapter 5: Working in Hollywood

You've got a job... now what?

If you follow the advice in this guide, before long you will have a job in Hollywood. And I don't mean taking orders at Bubba Gump Shrimp Company – I mean an actual paid acting job. If you think the business of Hollywood gets any less confusing and intimidating after you have been hired, think again. You have a whole new set of challenges to deal with. The purpose of this section is to give you an overview of the process that occurs between nailing the audition and reporting to the set for the first day of work. Before that though, we will tell you more than you ever wanted to know about Hollywood unions. Sorry, but it's something that you need to know.

Lawyer, lawyer, everywhere...

After you have been chosen for the part, the first order of business is to get the contract taken care of. If it is a union project (more on that soon) the standard contract from the union will be sent to your agent. If you don't have an agent the production company will send the contract directly to you.

This would probably be an excellent time to get an agent. It might very well be the first time that an agent you would consider hiring will actually talk to you – after all, you do have a paycheck coming. Trust me, when you get to the point where you start receiving contracts from the unions, particularly the Screen Actors Guild (SAG), you will be happy you have an agent to look it over.

While we are on the subject of SAG, let's spend a few minutes talking about the major unions that you will encounter in Hollywood.

The Screen Actors Guild is by far the most powerful and influential. SAG is the union that oversees projects shot with film. This covers the vast majority of mainstream commercial productions; including films, most television programs, and commercials. The primary purpose of SAG is to protect the rights of the actors. They have put together a dizzying array of contracts with more rules and regulations than anyone who isn't a lawyer would care to read. Some of the things that SAG contracts stipulate include:

Salary

This includes the minimum rate that everyone must be paid based on their role in the production. The rates vary from the principal performers at the top of the scale, to the extras and other roles such as voice over talent near the bottom of the scale. Performers or their agents can negotiate higher salaries, but SAG sets the minimum. By the way, don't expect to negotiate a higher than minimum salary until you have some leverage in the industry.

Lots of details about the production

This includes details such as whether it's a theater or television release; whether it is a national or international release; the dates of the shoot; who maintains rights to the name and likeness of the actor as well as merchandising rights. The list of what SAG covers goes on and on. Feel free to visit their website to learn more.

SAG is known as the most difficult of the unions to get into. Getting into SAG has become an art form over the years with several "back-door" methods used to gain membership. Some of the most popular include:

Taft-Hartley it – This is an expression you will hear a lot in Hollywood. It is actually very simple. Without boring you with the legalese, it refers to the situation we alluded to earlier in the guide when a union production wants to hire you. They fill out some paperwork and you are eligible. Simple pimple.

Extra, Extra - One of the favorite ways over the years has been to work as an extra on a union project. Union and non-union extras are usually hired for the same project. If you make friends with the right people on the set they may give you one of the union "vouchers" for the day. Get three of these union vouchers and you can join the union. Easy peasy. Hey, it was good enough for Brad Pitt so why not you?

Online and confusing - One way to get into the union that not everyone knows about is by taking advantage of the SAG provisions for new media. This allows anyone to produce a union program that is considered new media (web shows for example). Once they have a union project they can hire themselves. We invoke good old Taft-Hartley and you are right as rain, and eligible to join SAG.

If you do become eligible to join SAG it isn't cheap. The initiation fee is currently $2,277. Annual dues are $116 plus a percentage of your income.

While it may seem as if all of Hollywood is obsessed with SAG, there are two other unions that you will also encounter.

The American Federation of Radio & Television Artists (AFTRA to you and me) is the union that covers all productions made with tape. This represents a much smaller amount of projects; mostly consisting of reality television, talk shows, and the occasional soap opera. AFTRA offers similar protections to its members as SAG. If you want to join AFTRA you won't have the drama involved in joining SAG. Pay the $1,600 initiation fee and the $63.90 semi-annual dues and you are in. It almost seems too easy.

The third union that you will hear about is called Actors Equity Association (AEA). This is the organization in charge of theater productions. If you appear in a union theater production, it will be under the AEA contract. Basically, if you get a job in an Equity production you will be eligible. The dues are $1,100 for the initiation fee plus $118 per year.

While SAG takes up the majority of the conversation, both in Hollywood and in our guide, all of the unions essentially serve the same purpose. They all have contracts that stipulate everything involved in productions. Whether they are film, television commercials, theater, or new media, there are one or more contracts from the unions that stipulate all of the protections and rights of the actors. SAG in particular has a contract that seemingly covers every type of production, both by type and by budget.

Each contract has its own unique language and jargon. Contracts for commercials, for example, may have clauses that stipulate how crowd scenes and public events, which are commonly used in commercials, should be handled. I could go on for 100 pages about all of the differences in the various contracts (don't worry, I won't), but all you need to know is that everything about union projects is heavily regulated and mandated. On occasion the production company will add an additional stipulation or contract that an actor must agree to sign. This is common when the production requires a specific and unusual amount of secrecy about the project.

While union projects are highly regulated, non-union projects are pretty much anything goes. They still have to adhere to basic California employment laws, but other than that all bets are off. As we have mentioned before, if you are a union member you cannot appear in a non-union project. For everyone else though they can offer a great opportunity to work and (hopefully) make some money. Because virtually nothing about a non-union project is mandated it is very important that you negotiate what you can. You may not get a formal contract the size of a novel like you would for a union project, but you should get a booking info sheet with the pertinent details spelled out. Just remember, in a non-union project don't expect anything that isn't explicitly spelled out.

Back to our scheduled programming...

OK, with our lengthy digression about the unions over, we can get back to what you should do after you get the job. The first person to contact you will probably be the assistant director, or on a bigger project the second assistant director. They will give you all of the important details about when, where and how to get to the set. You will then hear from wardrobe and may be asked to come in for a fitting. Please take a shower. More than one wardrobe person has lamented working on actors with "questionable" hygiene. And it should go without saying by now, but be respectful and polite to the wardrobe people (and everyone else). This includes learning their name and not referring to them as "wardrobe."

You should have been emailed or sent a copy of the script by now. Your most important job is to learn the script and show up at the set ready to work. Of course, YOU WILL NOT BE LATE. If you are not positive where the location is, take a test run. Allow for L.A. traffic, which means plan to get there at least an hour before you need to. There is no excuse for being late, particularly as an inexperienced actor. People do not want to hear excuses.

Come to the set with whatever you have been explicitly told to bring (such as wardrobe) and nothing else. You can bring your cell phone, but turn it off before entering the building. Have a warm friendly smile when you enter the building. You're getting paid after all.

Getting Paid

It seems as if getting paid for your acting job should be a simple thing. And it often is. But, according to a survey of actors, a surprising number complain that their pay is often late, sent to the wrong place, or never comes at all. In this section we will take a quick look at how you are supposed to get paid, and what to do when your pay doesn't come as expected.

The Process

If you don't have an agent, the process of getting paid is straight forward. The production company pays you the agreed amount at the agreed upon time; nice, neat, no problem. You work on a film, or guest star in a television show or two and you get your money. If you have a large part that will last more than a week, you will probably get paid during the production. For small parts and those that are a few days or less, you will get paid after the gig.

If the job is a union project it is very unlikely that you will have a problem getting paid. If you do, that's what the union is for. It's mostly non-union jobs where the problems occur. Allow for the possibility that it was an honest mistake and your check wasn't sent or was sent to the wrong address. If you haven't received your pay a week after you should have, a polite call to the production company to find out the status is appropriate. Hopefully the issue is resolved, and if not you have a couple of choices.

You can hire an attorney, but in most cases this is not worth the trouble or the cost. You can also report the production to the Better Business Bureau. This most likely won't get you your money, but at least their behavior will be on record. If you are working with industry professionals it is very unusual for an intentional withholding of pay to occur, but stuff does happen. The best way to prevent this from happening is to do a little research on the production company before you take the job, but most actors are so happy to get work that they often don't do this.

The Agent said what?

If you have an agent you will be asked to sign a form authorizing the agent to cash your check. When you get paid, the agent will take out his commission and pay you the balance. When you get a job, the production company will be notified to send the check to the agent. Since this is standard operating procedure, they will have no problem doing it. While most actors agree to this, not all do. Many do not like the idea of the agent controlling the money in this fashion. The reality is that most actors don't want to make a fuss and they just go along with the way things are done. What should you do? It really depends on how important the issue is to you. Is it worth losing the agent or damaging the relationship? Most people don't think so, but only you can decide for yourself.

It's important to remember that whatever money you earn you will have to share with the partner in your acting career – The United States Internal Revenue Service.

Make sure to keep all paystubs and receipts. While you should always consult with an accountant, most items that you have purchased specifically for your acting career will be deductable. This can include everything from your marketing materials, to travel expenses, continuing education expenses, and many other items. It can't be over-stated; you must keep all of your receipts. If you ever get audited you will need them.

Chapter 6: Key Ingredients of a Successful Career

There are a lot of reasons why actors do not succeed in Hollywood. If you have absolutely no talent, nothing you read in this guide will make you a working actor. The reality though, is that thousands of people who do have talent, and had a legitimate opportunity to succeed, did not.

In examining successful actors, the reason why they found success where others failed becomes obvious. There are clearly defined qualities and actions that separate the working actors from the rest of the pack. We have talked about some of them in this guide. In this section we are going to list the actions that distinguish the wannabees from the actually are's. Simply put, the quality that leads to a successful career as an actor can be summed up in two words; "A PLAN."

Having any plan at all will put you in rare company among actors in Los Angeles. Having the plan that we outline here will give you the best possible chance for success.

As easy as 1,2,3…

You need money

Sorry to be the bearer of bad news, but it costs money to live in L.A. You better have a way to support yourself while you are pursuing your dream. There are many ways to do this. Some prefer the "classic" actor jobs such as waiter/waitress or bartender. These are still popular because they afford so much flexibility. Other work, such as assignments with temp agencies, can offer flexibility as well. Sales can also make a great career for actors. It rewards personality, can be flexible, and the pay can be great. One last job that doesn't get talked about a lot for actors is that of corporate trainer. I have known several actors who did very well in this field. They teach workshops in a variety of subjects to corporate clients. Many actors are naturals because they are so comfortable standing up in front of a group. The companies that hire you will train you in their specialty. I will include a couple of links in the resource section for this interesting and potentially lucrative career.

It doesn't matter exactly what you do, only that you have a source of income. If you don't figure this part out you will always be scrambling to survive.

You need these two things to be taken seriously as an actor:

You need experience - This is intimidating for many people, but it doesn't have to be. There are plays, student films, and independent films being cast and produced every day in and around Los Angeles. Over the next six months to a year get in as many as you can. By the end of that time, and perhaps much sooner, not only will you have some good credits to put on your resume, you will also have some material to put on a video reel. If you already have some or all of this done, you are ahead of the curve. Whatever you do, don't stop. Keep working these projects while you look for paid work.

You need training – The other thing that industry professionals want to see on your resume is training. We talked about this a little earlier, but it shouldn't be forgotten. Take a variety of classes. Work with the best teachers that you can afford. The added benefit to this is the camaraderie and networking opportunities.

When you have completed some film credits and respected training courses, you will be taken much more seriously by the industry.

Discover the power of Proactive Goal Setting

Before you run kicking and screaming from the room thinking "Oh no, not another goal setting lesson," let me stop you. This is goal setting unlike anything you have seen before. If you have ever tried to use goal setting you were probably instructed to write down all of the things you want to achieve in the next year, and the next five years, and so on. I used to do it this way as well and, with apologies to people who enjoy this activity, the exercise proved to be a complete waste of my time. I have always been a positive person, and I strongly believe in the power of positive thinking, but writing down everything I wanted made no difference.

In reality, this old way isn't really goal setting; it is actually "goal dreaming." You are saying that if I clicked my heels together right now and wished, this is what would happen. The problem with this exercise is, although it may give you something to shoot for, it doesn't tell you where to aim. You know where you want to be, but you still have no idea how to get there.

Proactive Goal Setting turns this process on its head. You use the same one year, three year, and five year time periods that you used before, but instead of ending with where you want to be, this is where you start.

Let's say your goal is to have a paid job within one year, have an agent and be a member of SAG by your third year, and have a principal role in a major studio film and have a steady six figure income by your fifth year. What you now do is reverse engineer the process. What are the absolute best actions you can take in each time period to give you the best chance of success? Write everything down and come up with an action plan. It may include items such as:

Send out 20 mailings per month to targeted agents and casting directors – You can do a little research and target the casting directors that are working on projects that use your "type." Take a similar approach to find agents who would be the best fit for you and touch base with them. When you send out your pictures you can include a little something to set you apart; maybe an article that would interest them; a great recipe, whatever you can think of that will add value.

Appear in at least six events per year with casting directors and agents in attendance. You can find acting classes and workshops that offer this opportunity all the time in L.A. Try to focus on the attendees that fit your overall plan the best.

Commit to asking friends and acquaintances to introduce you to at least five people every month who are currently working in the business; in any capacity. This business is about relationships. The more people you know, and who know you, the better chance you have of forming a relationship that will eventually result in work.

Commit to sending at least 10 electronic submissions every month. Mix them up between film, television, and commercials. You might find that the work comes from an unexpected source.

Commit to putting up your own website within the first year. This is easier than you think and can be very inexpensive. For a few dollars, you can have your own professional looking site up in no time. Go to YouTube and look up how to create a website with Wordpress. You will find tons of videos showing you just how easy this can be. You can put everything, from your headshot and resume, to video, to whatever else you can think of up on the site. Now when someone says, "why don't you send me your information?", you can give them your website address and they can see your info right away. If it is available, using your name is a great option for the domain name.

There are many other things that you can do. Talk to working actors and see what works for them. There are always new and creative opportunities.

The true power of proactive goal setting is that, unlike traditional goal setting, this process puts you firmly in charge. You know that your actions are putting you closer to your goal every day. Maybe you will get that big break during the first year, or maybe it will take longer, but you can know that you are not waiting to get lucky. You are making your luck. This is incredibly empowering. After the first year you can analyze your actions and see if any were particularly effective. Inevitably, you will find that some activities are simply producing better results than others. That's a good thing. Simply tweak the plan and spend more time doing what is working.

When you have taken a few hours and put together an action plan based on proactive goal setting you will be stunned at how quickly things start happening. Your overall results will increase exponentially. Instead of networking occasionally, or when you feel like it, it is now a part of your life. It doesn't require thought or mental energy. You simply do what is on the list.

At some point when discussing the business, people inevitably come to the question of how long it will take to succeed. The question is, of course, impossible to answer. There are so many unknown factors. When you approach the business with a plan though, you can truly see and feel the small successes that are leading to bigger ones. You don't feel like you are on a treadmill, because you are not. You are actively moving toward your goal.

As I wrap up this guide, my sincerest hope is that you realize the power of what you have just read. By all means go back over the material. This information has the power to give you the career in Hollywood that you want. I don't say that lightly. The strategies in this guide represent the best practices of those who are working and thriving in the business, along with advice from decision makers that are in the trenches every day. Sadly, most people who read this will think that it makes sense, and then get back to their busy lives. Hollywood does not reward those who are passive; you now have a plan that can work. Don't just sit there... use it.

Appendix – Online Resources

The Actors Voice – A fantastic site where veteran casting director Bonnie Gillespie answers common questions about the business. It's part of the Showfax website.

http://more.showfax.com/columns/avoice/

Breakdown Services – The homepage for the company that offers Showfax, actors access, & other valuable services. You will eventually use some of these services.

http://breakdownservices.com/

BizParentz Foundation – Though the site is targeted to the families of children in the business there are great resources for all.

http://bizparentz.org/thebizness/onlinecasting.html

acting answers – Wonderful site from actor David H. Lawrence. He answers a lot of the questions actors have about the business.

http://www.actinganswers.com

Mandy.com – Think Craigslist, but for the entertainment industry. Everything from casting information, to job listings, to classified ads.

http://www.mandy.com/

Backstage.com – Outstanding information about all facets of the industry. From the latest news to casting notices, you will find it all here.

http://www.backstage.com/bso/index.jsp

Playbill.com – Everything you ever wanted to know about the theater world. Purchase tickets, read the latest happenings, or watch video. It's all there.

http://www.playbill.com/

The American Society of Training and Development – Information for and about corporate training; also includes a section with job listings.

http://www.astd.org/

Langevin Learning Services – Training classes that prepare you to be a corporate trainer. They are pricey, but it can be a great job for aspiring actors.

http://www.langevin.com/

Cynopsis Media – News and information about the television and advertising world. Has an updated calendar with important industry dates.

http://www.cynopsis.com

Exploretalent – Large database of job listings for performers in a variety of fields; including actors, dancers, models, and musicians.

http://www.exploretalent.com/

Indieclub.com – news, casting information, and community that specializes in all aspects of film and filmmaking.

http://www.indieclub.com/

Getmoreauditions.com – service that submits headshots and resumes to producers, casting directors, and casting directors. Recommended by a number of industry professionals.

http://www.getmoreauditions.com/

Casting Society of America – Website for casting directors. Good to keep up to date on the latest happenings in the world of these important people.

http://www.castingsociety.com/

The Screen Actors Guild – Website for the most powerful and influential of the Hollywood unions. Lots of information about how the union works.

http://www.sag.org/

Internet Movie Database (IMDB) – Exhaustive list of movie information, including plot synopsis and listings of cast and crew. Pro version offers additional resources for actors.

http://www.imdb.com

Variety – Website for the respected industry magazine. One of the must visit sites for anyone wanting to keep abreast of the entertainment world.

http://www.variety.com

The Huffington Post – Entertainment page of the leading online news information site. News plus high quality feature articles.

http://www.huffingtonpost.com/entertainment/

TMZ.com – Couldn't leave it out. If you want to be up on the latest gossip, it's hard to ignore TMZ.

http://www.tmz.com/

Los Angeles Times Entertainment News – Extensive entertainment news and feature articles covering all aspects of the business. Interesting blogs provide important information.

http://www.latimes.com/entertainment/news/

BET – Focuses on the experience of the African American entertainment community. Interesting and relevant content.

http://www.bet.com/

Yahoo Movie News – Everything you ever wanted to know about the latest comings and goings in the film world.

http://news.yahoo.com/movies/

The Numbers – Fascinating site that analyzes trends and statistics for movies. See which movies dominated the market in particular years.

http://www.the-numbers.com/market/

The Wall Street Journal Movie Industry Page – Extensive news and financial coverage of the movie industry. Offers a different perspective than traditional industry sites.

http://topics.wsj.com/subject/M/movie-industry/3339

The Hollywood Reporter – Among the legendary trade magazines and websites for the industry. Covers all angles of the business of Hollywood.

http://www.hollywoodreporter.com/

Filmmaker Magazine – Follow the latest comings and goings from the world of independent film. Excellent resource for both film lovers and those wanting the latest info.

http://www.filmmakermagazine.com/

Billboard Magazine – Leading magazine that focuses on the music industry. Often finds overlap with other areas of entertainment industry.

http://www.billboard.com

Hollywood Scriptwriter – Interesting site that delves into the minds of the leading screenwriters. Fascinating and relevant for actors.

http://www.hollywoodscriptwriter.com/

Television without pity – Unique and fun look at a wide range of television shows. Very entertaining site that will make you laugh and tick you off as well.

http://www.televisionwithoutpity.com

Hulu – Offers many choices for television lovers. Full episodes of both current and past shows shown in a very user friendly format.

http://www.hulu.com/

www.ingramcontent.com/pod-product-compliance
Lightning Source LLC
Chambersburg PA
CBHW071414290526
45789CB00003BA/1478